A Reader's Digest Book

The credits and acknowledgements that appear on page 68
are hearby made a part of this copyright page.

Copyright © 2002 The Reader's Digest Association, Inc.

Library of Congress Cataloging in Publication Data has been applied for

ISBN 0-7621-0417-1

Reader's Digest and the Pegasus logo are registered trademarks
of The Reader's Digest Association, Inc.

To order additional copies of this book call 1-800-846-2100

For more Reader's Digest products and information,
visit our web site at rd.com

Printed in the United States of America

1 3 5 7 9 8 6 4 2

GEORGE W. BUSH

A HEROIC FIRST YEAR

By Jeffrey Rosenberg

Reader's Digest

THE READER'S DIGEST ASSOCIATION
PLEASANTVILLE, NEW YORK/MONTREAL

GEORGE W. BUSH

A HEROIC FIRST YEAR

BY JEFFREY ROSENBERG

*"I saw him shift, from being 'Mr. President'…
to the man chosen for this hour."*

—GWENDOLYN TOSE'-RIGELL
Principal, Emma E. Booker Elementary School, Sarasota, Florida

*"What a gentleman—the guy's a real regular guy.
He's a real regular guy."*

—BOB BECKWITH
New York City firefighter, retired

PROLOGUE

There are moments in a man's life when the gravity of the occasion can be energizing or overwhelming, awe inspiring or paralyzing. At these times, the people counting on him need to know what choice he will make. Will he embrace the challenge, or will the challenge debilitate him?

Usually, these are moments a man faces in private, or at most, surrounded by his family. But when that man is a public figure, the whole world watches.

George W. Bush, neat and respectful in a dark suit, white shirt, pale green tie, and lapel flag pin, had just descended from the marble lectern left of the altar at the National Cathedral in Washington, D.C. It was the National Day of Prayer and Remembrance, September 14, 2001. His words complete, he solemnly walked across the ornate tile floor, momentarily grasping the hand of a female minister sitting to his right, before taking his seat in the dark oak pew next to his wife, Laura.

Seated next to Laura was George Herbert Walker Bush, the 41st president of the United States. Never breaking his glance from the altar in front of him, "41," as the father is warmly referred to by the men and women who work in his son's administration, reached over and grasped the hand of George W. Bush. That was the moment.

◄ *Former President George Herbert Walker Bush, center, reaches over to his son, President George W. Bush, left, as Barbara Bush looks on during a National Day of Prayer and Remembrance service at the National Cathedral in Washington, D.C., Friday, September 14, 2001.*

We can't know what former President Bush was feeling. We suspect it was much deeper than fatherly pride, though certainly pride was a measure of it. But figuratively, we all grasped the hand of George W. Bush. We all said, "We're proud of you, Mr. President." And, even more importantly, at a time when our tears had not yet dried, we all basked in the strength and the love emanating from our young leader.

That was the moment we could see that George W. Bush, at some point in the three days since terrorists had attacked our country, using American civilians as weapons and killing more than 3,000 people, had decided that he and the American people would make history, not be brought down by it. We would shape events, not be molded by them. And he, the president of the United States, had decided that he would lead all of us in this century's first great defense of freedom.

"God bless America," President Bush concluded his remarks.

"God bless you, Mr. President," we all said to ourselves, each of us holding his hand for a brief moment in that oak pew.

BEFORE NORMAL CHANGED

F or half of America, the half that didn't vote for George W. Bush in the 2000 presidential election, it seemed fitting. Inauguration Day, January 20, 2001, was cold and damp in Washington. The skies were gray all day. A misty rain, sometimes a steady drizzle, fell on the capital.

The people who had tickets for the event had to walk blocks from their cars to their bleacher seats and got soaked, their shoes riddled with mud.

Some would say that mud and muck were what this election was all about. Certainly, the 2000 presidential contest between George W. Bush, sitting governor of the Lone Star State, and Vice President Al Gore was one of the most controversial in American history. Never before had so many counted on so few "chads," as the little punch-out tabs on the ballots in Palm Beach County, Florida, are called. Indeed, it's not an exaggeration to say that many governments around the world could not have survived 36 days of uncertainty about their future leadership.

The presidential election had come down to a contest of lawyers in Tallahassee, Atlanta, and, finally, Washington. It wasn't until the evening of December 12, 2000, when television reporters stood on the steps of the U.S. Supreme Court, frantically trying to interpret the Court's ruling, that Americans knew who had won this "longest election."

As George W. Bush prepared to take the oath of office on the steps of the U.S. Capitol that drizzly January day, many still

▲ *George W. Bush takes the oath of office from Chief Justice William Rehnquist to become the 43rd president Saturday, January 20, 2001 in Washington.*

questioned the "legitimacy" of his presidency. Pundits on twenty-four hour cable news channels continued to debate how he could possibly lead a nation so deeply divided by the election.

But lead is what he promised to do. And looking back with the perfect vision granted us by the passage of time, it seemed as if George W. Bush knew something that Inauguration Day, something few of us understood. Our new president appeared to recognize that America, for all it's prosperity, faced great danger.

Perhaps he was attempting to heal a nation divided by the difficult election. Perhaps he was preparing us for an unknown future he suspected would be difficult.

"We have a place, all of us, in a long story—a story we continue, but whose end we will not see. It is the story of a new world that became a friend and liberator of the old, a story of a slave-holding society that became a servant of freedom, the story of a power that went into the world to protect but not possess, to defend but not to conquer."

Further in his speech, he observed, "America has never been united by blood or birth or soil. We are bound by ideals that move us beyond our backgrounds, lift us above our interests, and teach us what it means to be citizens. Every child must be taught these principles. Every citizen must uphold them. And every immigrant, by embracing these ideals, makes our country more, not less, American."

And then, "But the stakes for America are never small. If our country does not lead the cause of freedom, it will not be led."

"America, at its best, is also courageous," he continued several moments later. "Our national courage has been clear in times of depression and war, when defending common dangers defined our common good.

"We will build our defenses beyond challenge, lest weakness invite challenge. We will confront weapons of mass destruction, so that a new century is spared new horrors."

"The enemies of liberty and our country should make no mistake: America remains engaged in the world by history and by choice, shaping a balance of power that favors freedom. We will defend our allies and our interests. We will show purpose without arrogance. We will meet aggression and bad faith with resolve and strength. And to all nations, we will speak for the values that gave our nation birth."

Today, so many months after September 11, we know the president meant exactly what he said.

He spoke that day, however, to millions of Americans still hurt by the controversial election, still questioning whether this was the man to lead, wondering whether he would only be keeping the Oval Office chair warm, so to speak, for the next four years. "I will live and lead by these principles: to advance my convictions with civility, to pursue the public interest with courage, to speak for greater justice and compassion, to call for responsibility and try to live it as well."

By Any Other Nickname, It's Texas Politics

Before September 11, the Bush presidency certainly dealt with consequential issues. It's just that we don't remember them. Everything before September 11 seems a long, long time ago—and unimportant, even trivial. Like nicknames.

George W. Bush came to Washington, believing that, in many ways, he could govern in the nation's capital as he had in Austin, Texas, where he was a popular Republican governor with a Democratic lieutenant governor. In Austin, his style was to reach across the aisle to work with, even embrace, Democrats.

In Texas, his charm played well. In Washington, he was warned that his down-home ways might be less effective. Many seasoned Washington insiders were sure they were about to witness a loveable misfit in the Oval Office.

President Bush promised that, after years of unending scandal, he would restore civility to politics. His across-the-political-aisle Texas hugs that worked in Austin would, he told skeptical reporters, work in Washington. It was time to stop partisan politics and start working together, he proclaimed. "We're going to rise above expectations," the *Washington Times* reported the President as saying. "Both Republicans and Democrats will do what's right for America. Things will get done."

He quickly got to work. In his first week in office, he invited 90 members of Congress to the White House for a series of policy meetings. He met with numerous others individually. And he gave

▲ *President Bush with his cabinet in the Oval Office in Washington, April 9, 2001.* First row, from left: *Secretary of Commerce Donald Evans, Secretary of Interior Gale Norton, Secretary of Defense Donald Rumsfeld, Secretary of State Colin Powell, President George W. Bush, Vice President Dick Cheney, Secretary of Treasury Paul O'Neill, Attorney General John Ashcroft, Secretary of Agriculture Ann Veneman, and Secretary of Labor Elaine Chao.* Top row, from left: *U.S. Trade Representative Robert Zoellick, Administrator of Environmental Protection Agency Christine Todd Whitman, Secretary of Education Roderick Paige, Secretary of Transportation Norman Mineta, Secretary of Health and Human Services Tommy Thompson, Secretary of Housing and Urban Development Mel Martinez, Secretary of Energy Spencer Abraham, Secretary of Veterans Affairs Anthony Principi, Director of the Office of Management and Budget Mitch Daniels, and Chief of Staff Andrew Card.*

out nicknames. The president referred to six-foot-four-inch George Miller, a Democratic member of the House from California and a potential adversary on education reform, as "Big George," for example. The president has never explained the nickname thing, but he seems to believe that good-humored monikers like "Big George" keep the political infighting from getting too nasty.

And the president reached far to the left, almost as far left as he could go. One of the first lawmakers invited to the Oval Office for coffee was liberal Democratic Senator Edward Kennedy of Massachusetts. Bush wanted his guest to see that he was using the desk once used by Senator Kennedy's brother, the late John F. Kennedy.

When the president addressed a joint session of Congress on February 27, 2001, he said: "I want to thank so many of you who have accepted my invitation to come to the White House to discuss important issues. We're off to a good start. I will continue to meet with you and ask for your input. You have been kind and candid, and I thank you for making a new president feel welcome.

"The last time I visited the Capitol, I came to take an oath on the steps of this building. I pledged to honor our Constitution and laws. And I asked you to join me in setting a tone of civility and respect in Washington.

"I hope America is noticing the difference, because we're making progress. Together, we are changing the tone in the nation's capital. And this spirit of respect and cooperation is vital, because, in the end, we will be judged not only by what we say or how we say it, we will be judged by what we're able to accomplish."

As he settled into the White House, relationship building was clearly of great importance to President Bush. It didn't seem all

▲ *President George W. Bush shakes hands with Senator Edward Kennedy of Massachusetts after signing the* **NO CHILD LEFT BEHIND ACT**, *an education bill, during a ceremony at Hamilton High School in Hamilton, Ohio, January 8, 2002.*

that important at the time, just a different style of politics, what with the nicknames and all. But George W. Bush's penchant for making the personal part of his politics would soon serve him well on the world stage.

In the meantime, in peacetime Washington, the president had an agenda to push. He ignored the unsolicited advice he was getting from everywhere that, because he had not won a mandate, he must govern to the middle—that he should not push the platform of "compassionate conservatism" upon which he campaigned.

But push his agenda he did. In many ways, he was saying to the American public, I told you what I would do when elected; now I'm going to do it. And if you don't like it, you can send me back to Austin in four years.

After a bit more than a week in office, the president sent his education reform agenda to Congress. The bill gave parents the choice to remove their children from public schools that fail to meet federal standards three years running. When that happens, federal funding would follow the student to whatever school the parents pick—public, parochial, or private. His plan called for $3 billion for charter schools. Charter schools are independent schools that are authorized and financed by public education institutions, but run by entrepreneurs for profit. They are meant to be successful alternatives to poorly performing public schools, but many have failed as badly. Bush's education bill included $5 billion to make sure every American student can read by the third grade, and it required mandatory testing for every public-school student.

With the help of Democrats like "Big George" and Senator Kennedy, a version of the president's bill, the No Child Left Behind Act, passed Congress and was signed into law in January 2002. Surely, a political scientist could study the path it took from White House proposal to law and find numerous factors that contributed to its passage. There's no doubt, however, that a big reason for its success is that George W. Bush has a unique view of politics: The person is even more important than the politician inside.

A Healing Tax Cut

The first time George W. Bush spoke to Congress was on February 27, 2001. As he strode into the House chamber to address a joint session of Congress about his first budget, it's hard to imagine how he felt. This televised speech also would be the first time he spoke directly to the American people since taking office. He knew that millions were still angry about the election. He knew that nearly every American was wondering the same thing. Could this man, whom only half the voters had chosen, lead the country?

"America today is a nation with great challenges, but greater resources," the president told Congress and the nation that evening. "An artist using statistics as a brush could paint two very different pictures of our country. One would have warning signs: increasing layoffs, rising energy prices, too many failing schools, persistent poverty, the stubborn vestiges of racism. Another picture would be full of blessings: a balanced budget, big surpluses, a military that is second to none, a country at peace with its neighbors, technology that is revolutionizing the world, and our greatest strength—concerned citizens who care for our country and care for each other.

"Neither picture is complete in and of itself. And tonight I challenge and invite Congress to work with me to use the resources of one picture to repaint the other; to direct the advantages of our time to solve the problems of our people. Some of these resources will come from government. Some, but not all.

"Year after year in Washington, budget debates seem to come down to an old, tired argument. On one side, those who want more

▲ *President Bush signs his $1.35 trillion tax cut bill Thursday, June 7, 2001, at the White House, fulfilling his campaign promise.*

government, regardless of the cost; on the other, those who want less government, regardless of the need. We should leave those arguments to the last century, and chart a different course.

"Government has a role, and an important role. Yet too much government crowds out initiative and hard work, private charity and the private economy. Our new governing vision says government should be active, but limited; engaged, but not overbearing."

Of course, Bush's speech that night is remembered for more than presenting a reassuring vision of leadership to the American people. It included the promise of a check in every mailbox.

"Some say my tax plan is too big. Others say it is too small. I respectfully disagree. This plan is just right. I didn't throw darts at the board to come up with a number for tax relief. I didn't take a poll or develop an arbitrary formula that might sound good. I looked at problems in the tax code and calculated the cost to fix them. To create economic growth and opportunity, we must put money back into the hands of the people who buy goods and create jobs."

The president's proposal called for a $1.6 trillion tax cut over ten years. When George W. Bush was campaigning for president, Democrats and even some Republicans attacked it as a "dangerous scheme." Now, the tax cuts had become so popular that Democrats and Republicans in Congress couldn't move fast enough to enact them into law.

On May 26, 2001, Congress passed the tax relief bill, and the president signed it two weeks later, The new law lowered tax rates and gave immediate refunds, up to $600, to taxpayers.

Spy Plane Down

Chhina Holding U.S. Fliers in 'Spy' Crash," the *New York Post* headline blared. April 1, 2001, marked the start of an eleven-day standoff between the two world powers.

With twenty-four crew members aboard, twenty-two of them U.S. Navy personnel, one an Air Force airman, and the other a Marine, the EP-3 reconnaissance plane made an emergency landing at a military airfield on China's Hainan Island. The four-engine turboprop plane had been crippled when a Chinese F-8 interceptor jet collided with it over international waters. The jet had been flying dangerously close—"aggressive" and "endangering" in the words of Admiral Dennis Blair of the U.S. Pacific command. The Chinese jet crashed into the South China Sea, the pilot lost and presumed dead.

For nearly two days, the United States had no contact with the crew. Later, crew members would tell of harrowing minutes as they frantically worked to destroy documents while Chinese military stood outside the airplane, ordering the crew to vacate.

"My reaction is the Chinese must promptly allow us to have contact with the twenty-four airmen and women that are there and return our plane to us without any further tampering," the president said. "I sent a very clear message, and I expect them to heed the message."

It wasn't until April 3 that U.S. officials were able to meet with the crew, who were being housed in a military building on the air base, and determine that all were safe.

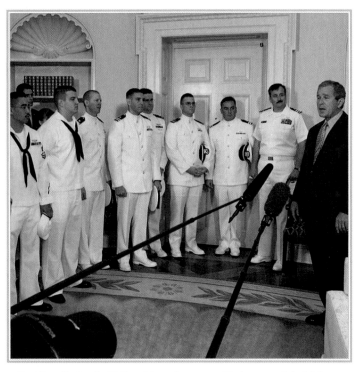

▲ *President Bush talks Friday, May 18, 2001, with the crew of the U.S. surveillance plane that made a harrowing landing on an island off China after colliding with a Chinese jet. The president gave the crew a tour of the Oval Office.*

For the next eight days, President Bush led a diplomatic high-wire act, working diligently to bring the crew home while ceding no moral ground to a Chinese government so clearly in the wrong.

On Wednesday, April 11, after the United States expressed being "very sorry" that the Chinese jet fighter pilot perished and "very sorry" that the spy plane made an emergency landing on Hainan without Chinese permission, the twenty-four crew members were released. The United States did not, however, apologize for sending spy planes up in the first place. The crew flew from Hainan on a chartered Continental Airlines Boeing 737 to U.S. territory on the Pacific Island of Guam. From there a military C-17 flew them to Hawaii.

President Bush received high marks for his first venture into high-stakes diplomacy. "He did exceptionally well—not just well, exceptionally well," Stephen Hess, a presidential scholar at the Brookings Institute, told the *Washington Times*. "To only appear when necessary and only say the minimum things necessary to be said was the perfect way to handle this. It was very Eisenhoweresque."

TEST PILOT IN
INTERNATIONAL WATERS

George W. Bush had little experience in international affairs. So he surrounded himself with men and women who did, people like Vice President Dick Cheney, Secretary of State Colin Powell, and Defense Secretary Donald Rumsfeld. And that became joke material for late-night television hosts, who portrayed Cheney as the man in charge. But in retrospect, the choice of advisors seems to suggest a new president confident in his leadership abilities, rather than a man in need of people to do his heavy lifting.

Still, coming into office, there was no question that George W. Bush was going to have to wade into international waters, and very soon.

His first meaningful interaction with Russia came in late March 2001, when he ordered nearly fifty Russians out of the United States in response to the arrest of FBI spy Robert Hanssen. Moscow responded by calling Bush's action a "throwback to the Cold War."

At about the same time, the president was using a harsh tone in dealing with China, taking Beijing to task for human rights violations and vowing to proceed with a Pacific missile defense system that the Chinese strongly oppose. And, of course, the spy plane incident was a fresh injury to U.S.-China relations.

Early in his term, President Bush was signaling that his approach to international affairs would be different from his predecessor's; he was much more willing to draw a line in the sand. "The message the president is sending is that his foreign policy is going to be based on reality," said White House spokesman Ari Fleischer.

▲ *President Bush laughs with Russian President Vladimir Putin as they answer questions from high school students during an assembly at Crawford High School in Crawford, Texas, Thursday, November 15, 2001.*

But what would that reality look like? Our allies in Europe were skeptical. Many of them viewed the president as uninterested in foreign affairs, as too much of an isolationist. They were nervous about the President's firm commitment to developing a missile defense shield. And they saw his decision not to go forward with the Kyoto treaty on global warming as a lack of concern for environmental issues. This was also about the time the federal government was preparing to execute Timothy McVeigh, leading many Europeans to think that this president—and most of the American people—were unbecomingly enthusiastic about the death penalty.

▲ *President Bush talks with British Prime Minister Tony Blair at the Palazzo Ducale, site of the G8 Economic Summit, in Genoa, Italy, on July 20, 2001.*

So this was the environment when George W. Bush took his version of reality across the Atlantic in June, as he embarked to Europe on what one aide told *Time* magazine was "the biggest trip of his life". His five-day tour included stops in Spain, Belgium, Sweden, Poland, and Slovenia—where he would meet, for the first time, Russian President Vladimir Putin.

He took his nicknames with him.

In Belgium, walking into his first meeting of NATO leaders, he slapped the just re-elected British Prime Minister Tony Blair on the back and bestowed upon him the nickname "Landslide," referring to the size of his re-election victory. *U.S. News & World Report* wrote that Blair was "delighted."

Washington Post columnist Jim Hoagland reported that the trip to Europe was a pretty good coming-out party for the Texan. "Bush showed a surprising grasp of and openness to European Union integration, including an enhanced defense role for the [Union]," Hoagland wrote. "He put his personal prestige behind a continuing U.S. troop presence in the Balkans. He gave a knockout speech in Warsaw on Europe in the last century, and unveiled his thinking about today's Russia being a part of Europe, not some distant evil empire, and pretty much like all those other countries."

Nothing, though, was more important than his first meeting with Vladimir Putin, which took place at Brdo Castle, just outside of Ljubljana, Slovenia, on June 16. It wasn't like the old days, when the United States and the Soviet Union were two superpowers staring at each other like heavyweight fighters before the bell for round one. But Putin still sits atop the old Soviet Union's nuclear arsenal. And Russia's influence in dangerous parts of the world is still significant.

Putin, by all reports, was pleased and impressed. President Bush had left the door open, if just a crack, for Russia to one day join NATO. It meant a great deal to Putin's political standing back home to have an American president clearly signal that Americans didn't need to see Russia as an enemy and, perhaps, one day could see Russia as a partner.

Said Bush: "I looked the man in the eye. I was able to get a sense of his soul. I wouldn't have invited him to my ranch," he said, if Putin was not somebody he felt he could work with.

In those five days of June 2001, George W. Bush was trying his wings as a statesman, testing his own brand of international diplomacy. He would need that experience soon enough.

★

RESEARCH SCIENTIST

C ritics have painted George W. Bush, the C-student from Yale, as something less than a rocket scientist. It was, therefore, ironic that an early issue of his presidency revolved around serious scientific research—blastocysts, pluripotent stem cells, and human cell specialization. And the first time he went on prime-time, national television, speaking to us in our living rooms, was to explain the ethical issues of this research as he saw them.

Time magazine suggested that the "president's stem cell decision could define his term."

"Perhaps no decision in his career has been so difficult for Bush," the magazine said, "possibly because it has the potential to reveal what kind of president he really is. A president who keeps his promises, come what may?"

During the campaign, Bush promised that federal funds would never be used to support research that involves the destruction of human embryos from abortion or in vitro fertilization. No matter the process involved, stem cell research requires doing just that. But it also offers science the possibility of preventing or curing some of man's most devastating diseases, such as diabetes, heart disease, cancer, and Parkinson's. Stem cells, because they have the potential to develop into any cell in the human body, can teach us how to turn off some types of cancer and allow us to permanently repair damaged tissue in the heart or spinal cord.

By late summer of 2001, a presidential decision had to be made. Researchers at leading universities were pressing for federal support. Private research labs were announcing that they had created or

▲ *President Bush meets Pope John Paul II for the first time at the pontiff's summer residence in Castel Gandolfo near Rome on Monday, June 23, 2001. The pope urged President Bush to bar the creation of human embryos for research, saying that America has a moral responsibility to reject actions that "devalue and violate human life."*

cloned human embryos solely for the purpose of research. And many in the evangelical community, in direct response, were clamoring for the president to keep his campaign promise.

It was indeed the first time Americans would see what kind of president George W. Bush was. This was a complex and emotional issue. Arriving at the proper decision demanded more than just reading poll numbers. By all accounts, the president did much more than consult pollsters. He spent weeks talking to members of Congress, scientists, researchers, doctors, patients' advocates, pro-life leaders, and even Pope John Paul II.

"I have made this decision with great care, and I pray it is the right one," the president said from his ranch in Crawford, Texas, the night of Thursday, August 9, 2001. He approved the use of federal funds to support research only on stem cells that have already been harvested from in vitro fertilization—approximately 65 stem cell lines worldwide.

The televised speech generated different reactions.

To many scientists, the decision was disappointing. Hundreds of scientists, including eighty Nobel prize winners, had petitioned the government to fund embryonic stem cell research. Some left the country to continue their work.

To Leon R. Kass, the University of Chicago professor named that night by the president to chair his new Council on Bioethics, it was a rare moment in presidential history. "I don't think one could recall a presidential speech, certainly not in my memory," he says today, "in which the president was a kind of moral teacher of the nation. The speech was really a model of moral pedagogy."

Time thought that Bush's speech presented a man deeply engrossed in the rigors of leadership, "as if to say, I am a man capable of subtle thought, not just ideological reflex; I can balance ways and means and right and wrong."

August 9, 2001—that was exactly 33 days before the world changed forever.

★

TERROR

For Gwendolyn Tose'-Rigell, the principal of Emma E. Booker Elementary School in Sarasota, Florida, Tuesday, September 11, 2001, was never supposed to be a normal day. Unlike the rest of us, when she woke up that morning, she knew this would be a very, very different day. Mrs. Rigell, as the students call her, knew that this would be a historic day for her school, her teachers, and her students. She just didn't know they would all play a role in world history.

▲ *President Bush listens as White House Chief of Staff Andrew Card informs him of a second plane hitting the World Trade Center while Bush was conducting a reading seminar at the Emma E. Booker Elementary School in Sarasota, Florida, September 11, 2001.*

For George W. Bush, Tuesday, September 11, 2001, was carefully laid out on his daily schedule, beginning with a visit to Emma E. Booker Elementary School. He was on time. He is almost always on time, wherever he goes. Indeed, reporters who cover him on a regular basis say that this may be the biggest difference between the Bush White House and the Clinton White House—efficiency that would make a nuclear clock proud.

"When he pulled up to the school, I knew nothing about what had happened," Mrs. Rigell says today. "All of the television sets at the school were set up for closed-circuit coverage of the president's visit.

"When he came in, he excused himself to make a phone call. After he made the call, he came back in, then greeted about six of us, including myself, the superintendent, some members of Congress, and our local teacher of the year. I went into the holding area with him, just the president, myself and the Secret Service agents. At that point he said, 'I apologize for having to leave to make the call, but a commercial plane has hit the World Trade Center.' "

At that point, according to the *Washington Post*, the president's aides were under the impression it was an accident involving a small, twin-engine plane. Of course, we now know that it was American Airlines Flight 11, a Boeing 767 out of Boston's Logan International Airport. At the time he was speaking with Mrs. Rigell, the president thought we were dealing with a terrible accident, nothing more.

◄ *The World Trade Center south tower, left, bursts into flames after being struck by hijacked United Ailines Flight 175, as the north tower burns following an earlier attack by a hijacked airliner in New York City, September 11, 2001.*

Shortly, the president and Mrs. Rigell left the holding area and proceeded into the classroom that he was scheduled to visit. The teacher was introducing her class of sixteen children to the president when Chief of Staff Andrew Card came across to tell him that the second plane had hit. "I was standing right next to him," Mrs. Rigell recalls.

At 9:05 a.m., United Airlines Flight 175, another Boeing 767, hurled through the south tower of the World Trade Center.

"I didn't know what the news was, but I figured it had to be something of great magnitude for his aide to come right across in front of live television cameras.

"I saw his lip quiver. He reached down and picked up a book. I was just thinking to myself, 'What could it have possibly been?'

"Then he told me there was going to have to be a change in plans, that it was terrorist in nature. He would have to leave. He apologized.

"At the time I remember thinking, my goodness, I'm principal over one school. I know how devastated I would be if just one of my children got injured or wasn't coming home. He must have felt, I thought to myself, as if he had children not getting home tonight. 'No need to apologize,' I told him. 'Whatever we need to do we have to make it work.'"

"You know," Mrs. Rigell recalled later, "we had been together the entire time. Something had to be inside of him. Because at that point … he went from being 'Mr. President' to … another level, to the man chosen for this hour. He didn't have enough time to think about what he was going to say or how he was going to respond. It was genuine. I saw compassion. I saw a very human side. I saw a man devastated that this happened on his watch."

The president left her to make a few comments to the press.

It was 9:30 a.m. when the president spoke to reporters before leaving the school. Just as Mrs. Rigell had seen in person, he

▲ A helicopter flies over the Pentagon on Tuesday, September 11, 2001, as smoke pours from the building following a direct hit by hijacked American Airlines Flight 77.

appeared shaken on national television. He called the morning's events "a national tragedy."

Then he said, "Terrorism against our nation will not stand."

By 9:55 a.m., the president was back on Air Force One, which

▲ *President George W. Bush addresses the nation from the Oval Office concerning the terrorist attacks at the World Trade Center and Pentagon on Tuesday, September 11, 2001.*

took off immediately from Sarasota Bradenton International Airport.

Just four minutes later, American Airlines Flight 77, a Boeing 757 that had taken off from Dulles International Airport in Virginia, not far from the White House, exploded into a fireball as it struck the side of the Pentagon. The president would find out later that Barbara Olson, the wife of Solicitor General Theodore B. Olson, was on that plane. Ted Olson was the man who had successfully argued the Florida election case on behalf of then-candidate George W. Bush in front of the U.S. Supreme Court.

As terrorism hit the United States, the president and his team were scattered. Secretary of State Colin Powell was in Peru; the chairman of the Joint Chiefs of Staff was in a plane over the Atlantic Ocean; and the president himself was in Florida. Back in Washington, the vice president and the president's top aides had been hustled into a concrete bunker underneath the White House by the Secret Service. Information was flowing in at a rapid-fire pace, but it wasn't always accurate. Still, decisions had to be made, and they had to made fast.

Transportation Secretary Norman Mineta ordered every airplane over U.S. territory out of the sky—there were 4,546 airplanes flying at that moment.

The Pentagon put jet fighter patrols into the air over Washington and New York, and ordered a fighter escort for Air Force One. AWACS radar and surveillance planes were put into the air over the East and West Coasts.

From Air Force One, the president gave a harrowing order. Any commercial airplane under the control of hijackers was to be shot down, regardless of the number of civilian passengers on board.

Very shortly, the vice president was informed that a jetliner was just eighty miles away, heading toward Washington. With the president's authority, he ordered fighter jets to engage the flight and, if necessary, take it down. Minutes later, both the president, in Air Force One, and the vice president, in the underground bunker, were told the plane had crashed in southwestern Pennsylvania, not far from Pittsburgh. It was nearly two hours before the Pentagon could tell them for sure whether the plane had crashed or been shot down by U.S. air-to-air missiles. (We know now that it crashed, and did so thanks to the heroics of several passengers on board.)

Confusing reports were hurtling into the White House and then to Air Force One. A plane went down near Camp David. A car bomb blew up in front of the State Department. An explosion ripped through the area surrounding the Capitol Building. The Old Executive Office Building, which sits on the White House grounds, directly next to the White House, was on fire.

All of these reports were terrifying. And none of them was true.

Most terrifying was a report—deemed credible at the time—that Air Force One itself was a target.

At 10:40 a.m., Air Force One was heading toward Washington. Then the vice president called. He urged the President not to return, not yet, that it was still too dangerous.

The president's plane turned west toward Barksdale Air Force Base in Louisiana.

When the plane landed, military personnel carrying automatic weapons immediately surrounded it. News reports said only that the president was at "an unidentified location in the United States."

At 12:36 p.m., President Bush stood before television cameras in a conference room off the Barksdale base commander's office. "The resolve of our nation is being tested," he said. "But make no mistake. We will show the world that we will pass this test."

Next, at about 1:30 p.m., Air Force One took off for Offutt Air Force Base in Nebraska, where there were secure facilities that

▲ *President Bush sits with his National Security Council during a meeting in the Cabinet Room of the White House on Wednesday, September 12, 2001. From left to right, CIA Director George J. Tenet, Secretary of Defense Donald Rumsfeld, Secretary of State Colin Powell, President Bush, Vice President Dick Cheney, Chairman of the Joint Chiefs of Staff General Henry Shelton, and National Security Advisor Condoleezza Rice.*

▲ *President George W. Bush speaks by telephone from the Oval Office at the White House in Washington with New York City Mayor Rudy Giuliani and New York Governor George Pataki on Thursday September 13, 2001.*

made it possible for the president to convene his National Security Council via a video hookup.

After the plane landed, the president, according to the *Washington Post*, told the Secret Service: "We need to get back to Washington. We don't need some tinhorn terrorist to scare us off. The American people want to know where their president is."

Arriving inside the U.S. Strategic Command headquarters at Offutt, the president was informed that they were tracking a commercial airliner from Spain heading toward the United States. The plane was transmitting an emergency signal, suggesting a possible hijacking. The president confirmed the order that, if they were sure, the plane had to be brought down. It turned out to be a false alarm.

Next, Air Force One headed home toward Washington, D.C. From the plane, the president placed a call to Ted Olson.

It was decided that the president would address the nation that evening from the Oval Office.

"One of the things I wanted to do was I wanted to calm nerves," the president would later tell the *Washington Post*. "I wanted to show resolve, and I wanted the American people to know a couple of things—one, that this was an unusual moment, but that we will survive, and we'll win."

That evening, the president appeared on national television.

"A great people has been moved to defend a great nation," he said. "America has stood down enemies before, and we will do so this time. None of us will ever forget this day. Yet we go forward to defend freedom and all that is good and just in the world."

Jane Watrel, an NBC television reporter, was at her home in

Alexandria, Virginia, just across the Potomac from Washington, D.C., when the first plane hit. "As soon as the second plane hit, I knew I had to get into work. A producer called me. She was telling me not to drive by the Pentagon, that traffic was too bad. She was talking to me on the phone, then she yelled, 'The Pentagon's been hit.'"

"That night, some of our stations wanted a piece for the eleven o'clock news on what happened in Washington. I had to go live from the White House. That's when things really started to hit me. That whole area was blocked off three blocks away from the White House. I parked. There wasn't a soul anywhere. It was eerie. I started walking up the street. I went through two or three ID checks. They checked my bags. They checked me. Then I noticed how dim everything was. They had dimmed all the lights at the White House. It was 10:30 at night and the White House looked like it was in a ghost town.

"I did my report and I left. It was eerily quiet. I drove home. Nobody was on the roads. On the way home, I noticed that all of the lights had been dimmed on all of the monuments."

Painstakingly Searching

The next two days, Wednesday the 12th and Thursday the 13th, were thick with anxiety. American families discussed whether to buy gas masks over the dinner table. And Americans were, quite frankly, not yet sure what kind of leadership they would find in George W. Bush. *Time* had, for example, called his Oval Office address of Tuesday night "uninspiring."

For President Bush and his top aides, these two days were filled with intelligence briefings, military planning, statements to the press, and working to build the international coalition that would support the war on terrorism. The president visited the Pentagon and the burn unit at the Washington Hospital Center, where he met victims of the Pentagon attacks who were severely burned.

On Thursday, the president spoke via telephone with New York City Mayor Rudy Giuliani and New York Governor George Pataki. Television cameras were invited into the Oval Office to film the exchange, which was broadcast live. It was a difficult moment; a conference call proved an ineffective way for the three men to communicate. The interaction was stiff.

But when the president hung up and took questions from reporters, he was more relaxed. "Well, I don't think about myself right now," he said, when asked how he was doing. "I think about the families, the children." He turned his head from the reporters, his eyes filling with tears.

"I am a loving guy and I am also someone, however, who has got a job to do. And I intend to do it. And this is a terrible moment. But this country will not relent until we have saved ourselves and others from the terrible tragedy that came upon America."

America Hears a Voice

It was raining, downright pouring, when the mourners entered the National Cathedral on Friday, September 14, the National Day of Prayer and Remembrance.

"We are here in the middle hour of our grief," the president began his remarks. "So many have suffered so great a loss, and today we express our nation's sorrow. We come before God to pray for the missing and the dead, and for those who love them."

For the first time Americans heard a firm steadiness and a gentle resolve in his voice. He had become both our healer-in-chief and our commander-in-chief.

"On Tuesday, our country was attacked with deliberate and massive cruelty. We have seen the images of fire and ashes and bent steel.

"Now come the names, the list of casualties we are only beginning to read. They are the names of men and women who began their day at a desk or in an airport, busy with life. They are the names of people who faced death, and in their last moments called home to say, be brave, and I love you.

"They are the names of passengers who defied their murderers, and prevented the murders of others on the ground. They are the names of men and women who wore the uniform of the United States, and died at their posts.

Pedestrians flee the area of the World Trade Center as the center's south tower collapses following the terrorist attack on the New York City landmark Tuesday, September 11, 2001. ▶

"They are the names of rescuers, the ones whom death found running up the stairs and into the fires to help others. We will read all these names. We will linger over them and learn their stories, and many Americans will weep.

"To the children and parents and spouses and families and friends of the lost, we offer the deepest sympathy of the nation. And I assure you, you are not alone.

"Just three days removed from these events, Americans do not yet have the distance of history. But our responsibility to history is already clear: to answer these attacks and rid the world of evil.

"War has been waged against us by stealth and deceit and murder. This nation is peaceful, but fierce when stirred to anger. This conflict was begun on the timing and terms of others. It will end in a way, and at an hour, of our choosing."

Presiding over the service were leaders of the major faiths and denominations, including Christian, Jewish, and Muslim. In the audience were former presidents Bill Clinton, Jimmy Carter, and, of course, George Herbert Walker Bush. Al Gore was there, as well, putting President Bush together with his former election adversary for the first time since Inauguration Day.

"We have seen our national character in eloquent acts of sacrifice," the president continued. "Inside the World Trade Center, one man who could have saved himself stayed until the end at the side of his quadriplegic friend. A beloved priest died giving the last rites to a firefighter. Two office workers, finding a disabled stranger, carried her down sixty-eight floors to safety. A group of men drove through the night from Dallas to Washington to bring skin grafts to burn victims.

"In these acts, and in many others, Americans showed a deep

commitment to one another, and an abiding love for our country. Today we feel what Franklin Roosevelt called the warm courage of national unity. This is a unity of every faith and every background."

And then the president concluded: "As we have been assured, neither death, nor life, nor angels, nor principalities, nor powers, nor things present, nor things to come, nor height, nor depth can separate us from God's love. May He bless the souls of the departed. May He comfort our own. And may He always guide our country.

"God bless America."

When the service ended, the mourners walked out of the cathedral into bright sunshine and blue skies.

That afternoon, President Bush flew to New York City to visit, for the first time, the site where the World Trade Center once stood.

▲ President George W. Bush addresses a crowd as he stands with retired firefighter Bob Beckwith, right, from Ladder 117 at the scene of the World Trade Center disaster in New York on September 14, 2001.

WELCOME, BROTHER

F irefighters are not firefighters to each other. They are brothers.
Retired firefighters—they're just older brothers.

Bob Beckwith lost a lot of brothers on September 11. But it was-
n't until Friday that he was able to go into the city. As he puts it:
"I knew we lost a lot of guys. I was just so taken aback. It took a
couple of days to straighten my act up and get down there."

His children told him not to go. "You're too old," they said. He
was 69 at the time.

"My wife said I was nuts, that I should let the young guys do the
work."

To his wife and children he said, "'I'm out of here.' And I went
down."

Bob Beckwith is a retired firefighter. He's been retired more than
eight years.

"I went down there because I worked with a lot of the brothers
whose sons are in the fire department.

"I got down to ground zero the morning of the 14th. I got right
to work. I went to the front of the bucket brigade. I got a shovel and
started digging. We had a lot of brothers down there.

"Around lunch time I saw a couple of guys I worked with. After
lunch, we found a pumper in the rubble." A pumper, he explains, is
a type of fire engine. "We got a crane operator to move the pumper
out of the rubble and push it out into the street. Then we went back
to work digging. We heard that the president was coming. Then we
heard that the president was here so we put our shovels down and

went out onto the street. Nobody was standing on the pumper. I couldn't see where the president was supposed to be, so I jumped up on the pumper. I was facing what I thought was the command post, where a tent was set up, and microphones.

"Then this gentleman came over. He asked me if it was safe up there. I said, 'Yeah.' He said, 'Show me. Jump up and down on it.' I did. Showed him it was safe. So the guy said, 'Somebody's coming over here. When they come over, you help him up, then you come down.' So about seven or eight minutes later he brought the president over. I grabbed his hand, helped him up and said, 'You OK, Mr. President?' Then I started to get down. The president said, 'Where you going? You stay right here with me.' "

Speaking to the men and women working at Ground Zero, that was not in the president's plans. So a bullhorn was found for the president. He took the bullhorn in his right hand and draped his left hand around Beckwith, who was still wearing his firefighter's helmet with a large "164" on the front, his goggles and breathing mask hanging around his neck.

"I want you all to know," the president started, before being told by someone in the crowd to turn the bullhorn up louder. "It can't go any louder," he said, evoking laughter from the crowd.

"I want you all to know," he resumed, "that America today is on bended knee in prayer for the people whose lives were lost here, for the workers who work here, for the families who mourn."

"Go get 'em, George!" one of the workers yelled.

"This nation stands with the good people of New York City," continued the president, "and New Jersey and Connecticut as we mourn the loss of thousands of our citizens."

▲ President Bush, center, New York City Mayor Rudy Giuliani, left, New York Governor George Pataki, second from left, Senator Charles Schumer (D-N.Y.), second from right, and New York City Fire Commissioner Thomas Von Essen, right, look toward the fallen buildings during a tour of the World Trade Center on Friday, September 14, 2001.

▲ As rescue efforts continue in the rubble of the World Trade Center in New York, President Bush raises an American flag while standing on a burnt fire truck with retired firefighter Bob Beckwith. Bush toured the disaster area on foot after getting a helicopter view of the devastation.

Then came the instant, the instant when practically every American stood behind this newly tested president.

"We can't hear you," a man hollered from somewhere off to the president's left.

"I can hear you!" President Bush yelled through the bullhorn. Laughter erupted from the crowd. Then cheers. "I can hear you. The rest of the world hears you. And the people who knocked these buildings down will hear all of us soon!"

Louder cheers erupted. Men were thrusting their clenched fists into the air. Then the entire crowd began chanting, "USA! USA! USA! USA!"

His arm still draped around Bob Beckwith, the president paused, listening to the patriotic chant.

"The nation sends its love and compassion to everybody who is here," the president said. "Thank you for your hard work. Thank you for making the nation proud. And may God bless America."

As the president began to step down from the pumper, somebody handed him a small U. S. flag, which he waved as he stood for a few more seconds atop the pumper.

A few minutes later, as the crowd engulfed Beckwith, a Secret Service agent found him. The president was trying to find him, he was told. Turned out the president wanted to be sure to give Bob Beckwith that flag.

"The guy's a real regular guy. He's a real regular guy," Beckwith says today.

To War

The task was enormous, the expectations very high. As George W. Bush entered the House chamber of the U.S. Capitol shortly before 9 p.m. on September 20, he was being called upon to make one of the most important presidential addresses in the history of our Republic.

He had been invited by the Speaker of the House to address a joint session of Congress shortly after the attacks. The president agreed, but said he would not come until he knew exactly what he wanted to say. Tonight, he knew.

"In the normal course of events, presidents come to this chamber to report on the state of the union. Tonight, no such report is needed. It has already been delivered by the American people.

"We have seen it in the courage of passengers who rushed terrorists to save others on the ground …. We have seen the state of our union in the endurance of rescuers, working past exhaustion. We have seen the unfurling of flags, the lighting of candles, the giving of blood, the saying of prayers—in English, Hebrew, and Arabic ….

"My fellow citizens, for the last nine days, the entire world has seen for itself the state of our union—and it is strong.

"Tonight we are a country awakened to danger and called to defend freedom. Our grief has turned to anger, and anger to resolu-

A shell of what was once part of the facade of one of the twin towers of New York's World Trade Center rises above the rubble that remains after both towers were destroyed in the September 11th terrorist attack. ▶

▲ President Bush addresses a joint session of Congress on Capitol Hill in Washington on Thursday, September 20, 2001. Seated behind are Senator Robert Byrd (D-W.Va.), president pro tempore of the Senate, right, and Speaker of the House Dennis Hastert (R-Ill.), left.

tion. Whether we bring our enemies to justice, or bring justice to our enemies, justice will be done."

Discussing what happened on September 11, he said, "Night fell on a different world, a world where freedom itself is under attack."

And he identified the enemy. "Americans are asking: Who attacked our country? The evidence we have gathered all points to a collection of loosely affiliated terrorist organizations known as al Qaeda…. Its goal is not making money; its goal is remaking the world—and imposing its radical beliefs on people everywhere."

The president addressed another issue in that speech: religious tolerance. "I also want to speak tonight directly to Muslims throughout the world. We respect your faith. It's practiced freely by many millions of Americans, and by millions more in countries that America counts as friends. Its teachings are good and peaceful, and those who commit evil in the name of Allah blaspheme the name of Allah."

This is a theme the president would repeat throughout the war on terrorism: Be angry at our enemies, but do not blame our friends, regardless of the faith they practice.

He warned the American people that this would not be a short war. "Americans should not expect one battle, but a lengthy campaign, unlike any other we have ever seen. It may include dramatic strikes, visible on TV, and covert operations, secret even in success."

The president laid out what has since become known as the Bush Doctrine: "Every nation, in every region, now has a decision to make. Either you are with us, or you are with the terrorists. From this day forward, any nation that continues to harbor or support terrorism will be regarded by the United States as a hostile regime."

▲ New York City firefighters watch President Bush's address to a joint session of Congress in Washington while at the Engine Company 8, Ladder 2 station in New York on September 20, 2001.

He called Americans to join in the mission. "Great harm has been done to us. We have suffered great loss. And in our grief and anger we have found our mission and our moment. Freedom and fear are at war. The advance of human freedom—the great achievement of our time, and the great hope of every time—now depends on us."

After leaving the dais, he came to Senate Majority Leader Thomas Daschle, a Democrat and potential presidential rival in 2004. The two men hugged.

On the afternoon of October 7, speaking from the White House, the president told the American people: "On my orders, the United States military has begun strikes against al Qaeda terrorist training camps and military installations of the Taliban regime in Afghanistan."

LEADING

Enjoying unprecedented popularity, President Bush went to work.

He prosecuted a war on terrorism.

Russian President Vladimir Putin visited the President at his ranch in Crawford, Texas. Together, they visited a local school

He announced that the United States would withdraw from the outdated Treaty on the Limitations of Anti-ballistic Missile Systems with Russia.

The United States and Russia agreed to begin formal talks on steep cuts in strategic nuclear weapons.

He threw out the first ball for Game Three of the World Series at Yankee Stadium.

He publicly refused to accept any tax increases from Congress.

He named the headquarters of the U.S. Justice Department after Robert F. Kennedy.

He signed a $343.3 billion defense bill designed to deliver on his campaign promise to strengthen our armed services.

And he prepared for his first State of the Union address.

"In four short months our nation has comforted the victims, begun to rebuild New York and the Pentagon, rallied a great coali-

Fans at Yankee Stadium in New York watch President Bush speak prior to the start of Game Two of the American League Division Series on Thursday, October 11, 2001. The president's news conference delayed the start of the game between the New York Yankees and the Oakland Athletics. ▶

tion, captured, arrested, and rid the world of thousands of terrorists, destroyed Afghanistan's terrorist training camps, saved a people from starvation, and freed a country from brutal oppression," the president told the nation on January 29, 2002.

"The American flag flies again over our embassy in Kabul. Terrorists who once occupied Afghanistan now occupy cells at Guantanamo Bay. And terrorist leaders who urged followers to sacrifice their lives are running for their own."

It is impossible to judge a presidency in its second year. But the extremist Taliban is out of Afghanistan and there are Afghans who are going home after twenty years in refugee camps in Pakistan. There is an international force, shortly to be headed by a Muslim army from Turkey, trying to keep the peace around Kabul. There is an interim Afghan government looking into ways to rebuild the infrastructure and economy of this strife-torn country.

September 11, 2001, was a wake-up call for the United States and its new president. Americans have responded to George W. Bush's leadership during the difficult aftermath. He has certainly had a heroic first year.

Marine Corporals Gonzalo Corridori of New York City, left, and Jonathan Reynoso of Providence, Rhode Island, stand on the roof to view a giant American flag flown over the Kandahar International Airport in Afghanistan on Tuesday, December 18, 2001. The flag was signed by scores of well-wishers and was given to a Marine in New York following the World Trade Center attack. The flag was also signed by relatives of victims and rescue crews from the New York City Police Department and New York City Fire Department. ▶

ABOUT THE AUTHOR:

J effrey Rosenberg is a writer who knows how Washington, D.C. works. He worked in the administration of George Herbert Walker Bush. His credits include *The Better Homes and Gardens New Father Book*, as well as numerous columns and articles that he has written for politicians, policy makers, and athletes.

PHOTO CREDITS

Cover Photos by Corbis Sygma / Corbis Sygma **6:** Corbis Sygma / Corbis Sygma **8:** AP Photo / J. Scott Applewhite **12:** AP Photo / Doug Mills, Staff **16:** AP Photo / White House, Paul Morse **18:** Reuters NewMedia Inc. / CORBIS / Win McNamee **21:** AP Photo / Ron Edmonds **24:** AP Photo / Ron Edmonds **27:** AP Photo / Doug Mills **28:** Reuters NewMedia Inc. / CORBIS / Win McNamee **31:** AP Photo / Arturo Mari **33:** Reuters NewMedia Inc. / CORBIS / Win McNamee **34:** Reuters NewMedia Inc. / CORBIS / Sean Adair **37:** AP Photo / Heesoon Yim **38:** AP Photo / Doug Mills **41:** AP Photo / Doug Mills **42:** AP Photo / Doug Mills **47:** AP Photo / Amy Sancetta **50:** Reuters NewMedia Inc. / CORBIS / Win McNamee **53:** AP Photo / Doug Mills **54:** AP Photo / Doug Mills **57:** AP Photo / Shawn Baldwin **58:** AP Photo / Win McNamee **60:** AP Photo / Matt Moyer **63:** AP Photo / Ron Frehm **65:** AP Photo / Dave Martin